MY STORY AS A JENA 6

by

Bryant Ray Purvis

Based on a true story

PREFACE

When I was seventeen years old, I was charged with attempted murder. It was a crime I did not commit; in fact, I wasn't even in the room when it happened. But I was soon implicated as a conspirator, and from that moment on, my life changed forever.

I should have known that it was only a matter of time before either myself or someone I cared about would be hurt by living in Jena. White people stayed on one side of town, and black people stayed on the other. If you didn't follow these unwritten rules, then someone was going to get hurt. But I was an optimist kid, and all I cared about was hanging out with my friends, being good to my mom, and playing ball. I didn't understand at the time that there were people in the world that would attempt to ruin a black man's reputation, or even take his life, just to prove a point.

Eventually I had no choice but to leave my hometown of Jena. I moved to Dallas and discovered a whole new life. The people were progressive and educated, and I was accepted. However, even as I began to build a new life for myself, the attempted murder charge and ensuing court dates continued as the victim and his lawyer continued to pursue a conviction against me and five other black men, who became known as the Jena 6.

Now that I'm a few years older and can look back and reflect on the whole situation, I can see that there were egos involved, mixed with a sense of entitlement on behalf of the victim and his family. I don't blame them anymore for what happened to me during those years. I wasn't perfect myself. But mostly I can see now that ignorance breeds hate, and the only antidote is forgiveness.

I would not be the man I am today without having gone through this legal battle. I saw the good in people, and I saw the bad. And I learned that even if the opportunities we have in life are not equal, it doesn't mean that we can ever stop fighting for equality. It taught me to question authority, to stand up for what I believe in, and above all to fight to expel ignorance.

I'm proud to say that I graduated college and have started my own business. Now that I no longer have to keep looking behind me to prove my innocence, I can focus on the future and life outside of being a Jena 6. The future looks bright, indeed.

CONTENTS

MY BOOK IS DEDICATED
TO THE PEOPLE
WHO SUPPORTED THE JENA 6

THANK YOU.

LIFE IN JENA

Young men need more models, not critics.

—John Wooden

It was in the school gym where the district attorney attempted to bring a level of peace back to our shattered school. He had made a comment that several witnesses later said he directed at one group over the other. When he was questioned later, he dismissed the perception of the witnesses as incorrect. However, when two witnesses said I was in the area of an unfortunate attack, he not only held their testimony as valid but extended what they said as reason enough to arrest me for attempted murder.

While the magnitude of the offenses was vastly different, the number of witnesses for his offense was far greater. With only two witnesses who said they saw me there, but not as a participant in the crime, I was subjected to the fullest extent of the law.

Jena, Louisiana, is a small rural segregated town deep in the heart of Central Louisiana. The general population is a little below 4,000 people. White people live on one side, and black people on the other. We have separate hangouts, different parties, and segregated parks. It isn't written in stone, but Jena is just a segregated town.

Although the town was segregated, everyone went to the same schools—elementary, junior high, and high school—as part of the LaSalle Parish school system. Our schools were really old.

We had the first-style desks made completely out of wood. The schools had to be over a hundred years old.

We had seven period classes in high school. During school breaks, students would group on walkways or stairwells. We'd make rhymes or just clown around. We were interrupted by the teachers telling us to break up and separate even when no harm was being done. It seemed as if they didn't want to see us have any fun. When there was a fight at school, everybody would rush to the scene, then the teachers would rush in and break it up before things got serious. It was over quick. Punishment for fighting was a couple of days in in-school suspension.

In-school suspension was like a prison. It was a small room with wooden cubbyholes, each with a desk and a chair surrounded by three walls. The instructor would come around and drop off your day's work. After eight hours of not being able to speak, stand, or anything, you were allowed to leave. They made sure you never wanted to visit there again. I had my share of times in there for petty reasons. I hated that place!

Racism wasn't really an issue among the students, unless there was an altercation and the word "nigger" was thrown around! There were strict rules for us black students. We weren't allowed to wear certain color shirts; we couldn't wear earrings. They even minimized certain haircut styles that we could have, all because school staff said it was gang related. We had to tuck in our shirts and wear a belt with everything.

Whites, on the other hand, could wear steel-toe boots, bring a knife on a key chain, and even bring tobacco on campus.

Dating was always a big thing. The townspeople didn't approve of dating outside the race. Not meaning there was a consequence for doing so; it was just looked down upon. There was always a handful of rebellious people who did it anyway, but it would never last because of their families. They couldn't be seen in public together. But not everybody was racist. There were a few families that were genuine and didn't care about color. We actually visited each other's neighborhoods and houses. We dated and hung out with anybody, but that was a very rare occasion.

The only thing Jena residents had in common was Friday night football. That was always the highlight of the year.

Game days were like no other. We would get to school early to watch video of our opponents, and as the day went on, we couldn't wait until our last period so we could go to our field house. Sometimes our teachers would let us football players out early to go down to the field.

Our field house was a small room with wooden lockers and square cubbyholes along the walls. The school would prepare a nice pregame meal before every home game. Sometimes a local restaurant would cater our meals on special occasions. Before leaving for a game, Coach would turn off all the lights, and we'd all take an hour nap before preparing for the game.

Friday nights were the only nights when I felt Jena was a whole: the people and the town. I remember as we ran out of our dressing room onto the field, busting through the paper walls made by the cheerleaders, the crowd would go nuts. It was segregated, of course: three-quarters of the stands were occupied by whites, and one small corner by blacks. Still, they were all the best fans ever. They screamed and cheered for their Jena Giants every night! That had to be the only time Jena ever saw blacks and whites really interact.

Jena was divided by income. There was the rich neighborhood, which we called Snob Hill, where the white lawyers, doctors, and wealthy businessmen of Jena lived. I remember driving through Snob Hill, mesmerized by the nice houses and clean-cut lawns. I dreamed of living there someday.

The next neighborhood was Nebo, deep into the town of Jena, with acres and acres of land and cattle. The families in Nebo were country folk. They wore cowboy boots, Wrangler jeans, and Stetson hats.

Black people didn't go near Nebo, but when they did, it was in and out. There were all kinds of crazy stories about blacks who went in and never came out and about the things white people did to them. There was one particular story about a black man who had some white friends he liked to hang out with in Nebo. One night one of the white boys got mad because the girl he liked, liked the black guy. Long story short, that black man ended up dead. He was found in an oil pond with his penis in his mouth. No one was ever convicted of the crime.

Goodpine, Yearby Hills, Golden Hills, and Tarver Park were black neighborhoods. They were rundown, low-income areas. Goodpine, where I lived, was a small area with eight blocks of houses crammed together side by side. Everybody knew everybody. As a kid, I thought growing up in Goodpine was the greatest place in the world. My mom, Tina Jones, a single parent, always made sure my brothers and I had the best of everything. But with that came strict rules. She demanded good grades, neat appearance, and courteous manners. She made sure we were well dressed and clean-cut. She gave us just about everything we asked for, but at the same time, she expected a lot out of us. She taught us good manners like "yes sir, no sir, yes ma'am, no ma'am," always respect your elders, and be a gentleman. She was strict!

She stayed on me about my grades and about always doing my best. I wasn't a big fan of school early on in my childhood. I remember when I had to bring my graded papers home at the end of the week for my mother to see. I would ball up all the papers with bad grades, throw them under the seat, and leave them on the bus, thinking I was getting away with something. But by the end of the six-week period, my report card would show the truth. Mom would see the Ds or Fs, and I'd be in big trouble. I remember one time when the bus driver cleaned his bus and found my papers, and he called my mother. It was the worst! Mom took away all my privileges. I had to go to bed early while all the kids on the block were still outside playing. My friends laughed and made fun of me. Eventually I grew up and started taking school more seriously.

Mom liked a tidy house. There was hell to pay if we didn't clean up after ourselves. And every four days Mom would make us thoroughly scour the house from top to bottom. We mopped, dusted, swept, washed walls, and scrubbed the bathroom.

Mom didn't cook much. She bought lots of frozen foods that I could deep fry or put in the oven. Because I liked to eat a lot, I learned to cook at an early age. I went from eating frozen meals to cooking my own food. I got pretty good at seasoning food and making whole meals. I cooked just about every day.

Summers were the best. No school. And everybody, maybe twenty kids in our neighborhood, would all get together and play sports. We played kickball, baseball, basketball— you name it. We also played football in a huge field in front of my grandmother's house. It wasn't normal football; we played more like the old PlayStation game NFL Blitz. The older kids would kill us out there. They slammed and threw us around, believing it would make us tough.

But of all the sports, basketball was my favorite. I played for hours, sunup to sundown. I had my own dirt court in my yard.

One summer my dad got a steel pole and made a backboard out of an old basketball goal. He dug a hole, bolted it down, and made a basket. Everybody played at my house. We all believed we would make it to the NBA. When we first started playing, the court was half dirt, half grass. After playing on it for about a week, my mother's whole front yard was dirt. Mom wasn't happy, but it got us out of the house, so she made do and let us play.

I remember coming in the house after playing ball all day, covered from head to toe with a thick layer of black dirt from the court. My bath water would be black, and the ring around the tub had to be scrubbed every night. Mom hated it. Eventually, she started limiting my time on the court.

Because Jena was segregated, we never saw white people unless we were at school or traveled out of our neighborhood into town

I had a huge family. My grandmother and grandfather had six boys and six girls. And since my grandmother babysat us when Mom went to work, I spent a lot of time with my uncles. They taught me a lot growing up. We hunted, fished, rode four-wheelers, walked barrels—we did it all. I remember the old house next to my grandparents' house that had only one room standing. My uncles got a fifty-gallon barrel, tied it on both ends to a beam, put a saddle on it, and buckled it down. I got on that thing, and they threw me around. We were pretending I was riding a bucking bull, counting the seconds before I fell off onto the mattress below.

My uncles were smart. They cut hair as a hobby and got pretty good at it. As I got older, I wanted my hair cut all the time. They were never available or always had an excuse. So one time I built up enough nerve to cut my own hair. I messed it up so bad. I had bald spots and uneven sections. But the laughter and mockery didn't stop me. I was eager to learn. For months I walked around with messed up haircuts. Eventually I got really good at it. In fact, my haircuts looked so good, people started asking me to cut their hair. Soon I was cutting hair in our car garage every day, making seven dollars per haircut. I became the neighborhood barber. I did haircuts for children and adults. I was surprised that people trusted a teenager to cut their hair, but in reality we didn't have a barbershop on our side of town.

As much as I loved my uncles, I loved my grandmother more. I was really close with her. She taught me how to play every board game there was. I loved her cooking; she made the best homemade biscuits. I would beg her to cook breakfast for me. She died when I was young. When I lost her, it was one of the worst days in my life.

THE NOOSES

The more concerned we become over the things we can't control,

the less we will do with the things we can control.

—John Wooden

On August 2006, in the school courtyard during lunchtime, my life changed and my world turned upside down. I was sitting with a group of guys on the benches on the school patio. We were just shooting the breeze when a group of white students wandered over to the courtyard and sat on the benches under the big tree. It was no big deal. It had always been that way. Almost all the white students sat under the tree with the picnic benches, and most of the black students sat under the walkways and by the steps right in front of the academic wing. It was never stated or written in stone; it was just something that we did naturally.

On that day, for some reason, one of the students wanted to know if we "black students" could sit under the tree. We talked about it for a few minutes, not giving it any serious thought, when the principal happened to walk by.

"Principal Berk," the student called out to him.

"Yes?" he answered, walking over.

"Can we sit under the tree on the picnic benches?"

"It's a free country. You can sit anywhere you want," he said.

Curious about it all, after about fifteen minutes we all decided to go have a sit-down under the infamous "white" tree. As we approached the tree, we noticed many of the white students

13

leaving. Once we sat down, there were only a few white students left, and they were the guys we played sports with.

Nothing happened. Just some of the white students left the scene; there was really nothing to it.

The next morning, as we all arrived at school, there were two nooses hanging from a branch on the big tree in the courtyard. It triggered instant tension, and an incredible amount of indignation among all the students. The school staff hurried to take them down, but by then a heavy stir had already begun. Everybody was talking about it. Nobody knew who was responsible, but the results were unmistakable: total confusion, frustration, and fear.

A few hours later the principal announced that three white students admitted to hanging the nooses. As details emerged, they insisted that it was not a hate crime, nor a message being sent to black students sitting under the tree the day before. They said they were inspired by a scene from *Lonesome Dove*.

For the past month or so, students from Jena High School, Winnfield High School, Caldwell High School, and LaSalle Parish High School had been playing pranks on one another. They had been doing stupid things like teepeeing, trashing, and vandalizing buildings. So when the confession of the three white students didn't settle things, the authorities tried to make everyone believe the nooses were just another bad prank. However, the pranks had been directed at the school itself and had already been stopped. The nooses were specific.

Outraged, the black families protested. But Jena High School and the disciplinary committee concluded it was just a prank and placed the three white students on supervised school suspension for five days.

The following day, during the lunch hour, the black students organized a protest. We all sat together under the tree. A lot of white students took offense, and the situation got even worse. Fights broke out among both groups. The black students decided to continue the sit-ins every day, and every day a fight broke out during lunch and in the hallways. This went on for weeks.

It was so bad, there were at least two cops and a dog in every hallway throughout the school. Our school was now like a prison. Parents were afraid for their kids to attend school, so much so that although Jena averaged about 450 students, there were days when we barely had over a hundred. Fewer and fewer students attended each day. One morning about five minutes before lunch, the principal came over the intercom and announced, "The school is on lockdown! No one can leave or enter!" After all the doors were locked, we saw the narcotic police, bomb squad, and police dogs roaming through the halls, searching the entire school.

Hours later we found out that someone had called in a gun threat to the school. When they didn't find anything, the principal called an emergency assembly in the auditorium. I remember walking in, and it seemed like every police officer in LaSalle Parish was at the assembly. It was like walking into a courtroom. Our principal opened with a few words, then handed the microphone to the town's district attorney. Just like the school yard, the auditorium was segregated. All the white students sat on the south side, and all the slack students sat on the north side. So when the district attorney spoke, he addressed the black students.

"This has to stop," he said. "I can be your best friend or your worst enemy." Then he pulled out a pen and held it up for us to see. "I want you to understand, I can end your life with a stroke of a pen. The next person that gets into a fight, I will make an example out of them." His threat really calmed the tension, and it gradually dissipated. A couple of days later, the three white students responsible for hanging the nooses came back to school. Everyone watched as they strutted around campus, grinning and laughing.

It was November, football season, and the citizens of Jena loved football. Our team was the Jena Giants, led by two of the Jena 6 members. The team was having its best season in years and was bringing in big crowds to the games. One night, after losing to Winnfield, Coach got on the bus and said, "I better not hear another word, not even if you're dead!"

One teammate asked, "How you gonna say something if you're dead?" Coach got so mad at all the laughing, he threatened to run us when we made it back to school. Late that night, after we got back, we unloaded the bus and made our way home. The next morning, I got a flurry of text messages saying that school was canceled. I jumped up and got dressed, then hopped onto my uncle's motorcycle and rode to the school. As I approached, I saw black plumes of smoke and flashing emergency lights. Our school was on fire. I had a rush of mixed emotions.

School was canceled for five days. During that time, a white student gave a party at the local Fair Barn. One of my friends, Ron Barkley, received a cell phone message from a girl he knew, inviting him to attend. With nothing better to do, he decided to go with some other friends and check it out. When they arrived, there was a sign on the door, "No niggers allowed." Standing at the door, they were approached by a white man who asked, "Are you Ron Barkley?" Without waiting for an answer, he struck Ron full force on the jaw. Then Ron and the others were brutally attacked by more white students attending the "party." Adult chaperones eventually broke up the fight, and the police were called in. But by this time Ron had been kicked, punched, and hit over the head with a beer bottle. When the police arrived, they told Ron and the others, "You need to get back on your side of town." And left it at that.

The next day, the young white man saw Ron and his friends coming out of a convenience store and quickly retreated to his truck. Ron saw him and a scuffle ensued. The guy pulled out a pistol-grip sawed-off shotgun. He and Ron wrestled for control of the weapon. Ron and his friends were able to get the shotgun away from him. The man drove off, and Ron and his friends ran off with the weapon.

That following Monday was surreal. The school reopened with the main building and academic wing destroyed, and we were still reeling from losing the game and from the fight at the Fair Barn over the weekend. Tension was incredibly high.

Everything at the school was blocked off. We had makeshift classrooms in the school gym, auditorium, library, and basically anywhere that had four walls. To make matters worse, classes were crowded, and period bells weren't working properly. The whole thing seemed unreal.

Then things got worse. It was December 4, 2006. Every conversation on campus either centered on the school's arson, the Fair Barn fight, or the altercation at Gotta Go convenience store. The students were polarized. The black students saw it one way, and the white students saw it another way. The atmosphere was so bad we were all told to report to the gymnasium instead of the school square. So we all packed in the stands and talked among ourselves, segregated of course. And if you listened carefully, you could hear the black students saying they had had enough; revenge was the way to handle it. At one point, I heard someone say, "When the teacher says 'go to class,' let's rush the other side and just start fighting every white person in sight!"

That was the plan.

My first thought was of the district attorney's threat. So I made up my mind; I just wasn't up for that plan. So when the teachers announced it was time to leave for class, everybody got up and headed out the door. I ducked out and went in the other direction. Coming out of the gym, we gathered along a ramp outside the far door and waited for the fallout.

But there were no fights! People were leaving the gym, talking as they walked to class. Teachers on duty were telling us, "If you don't go to class, your name will be written down and sent to the principal's office."

I told the guys, "I'm out." So my girlfriend, her sister and I headed for class. We were halfway up the steps when we heard a loud *pop*. I turned around to see what it was. Groups of students rushed to the gym door. The crowd was so big, I couldn't see anything else. I jumped on top of the ramp near where I was standing to try to get a better look. I saw teachers and staff rushing to the scene. After a few minutes, I could see a guy laying on the ground. Suddenly, the teachers started yelling for everyone to go to class immediately!

The whole school was on the edge. Nobody knew what had happened. Emotions were so high, some students were crying. Even the teachers looked extremely upset. People kept asking what had happened. Our teacher was so upset she yelled at us to shut up and keep quiet!

When school let out, I didn't see any of my friends. When I got home, even the old people in our neighborhood knew what had happened. My friends Ron Barkley, Calvin Jameson, Tim Sherman, Marcus Bates, and Jeffrey Berk had been arrested for jumping John Bleacher.

It was all anybody could talk about. John had been rushed to the hospital for a black eye and minor bruises on his face. After just a few hours of treatment, John was released from the hospital. John was later seen at our school's ring ceremony that very night.

The next day, when I arrived at school, there were three policeman outside, talking among themselves. I felt uneasy as they were staring at me, watching until I entered the building. At one point our head basketball coach approached me. "Did you have anything to do with the fight the day before?"

"No!" I told him, then left for class. I wondered why he had asked that question, and it lingered in my thoughts for most of the morning.

After third period everything seemed normal. I was finishing up a worksheet when a knock at the classroom door caught our attention. It was the principal. He asked the teacher if he could see me in the hallway. Fear and dread gripped me. *What is this about?* I thought, as I got up and went to the door. To my surprise, he wasn't alone. Ten police officers and a police dog were waiting in the hall. As soon as I stepped out, a policeman read me my rights, put me in handcuffs, and ushered me out of school.

LIVING BEHIND BARS

It's OK to make mistakes. That's how we learn. When we compete, we make mistakes.

—Kareem Abdul-Jabbar

It was a long walk from the classroom to the squad car. I was speechless as my schoolmates watched nervously as I passed them. My mouth was dry, but my palms were sweaty. My mind was blank, but my nerves were on edge. The policeman gripping my arm wouldn't look at me. The principal looked down at his feet, never once looking up at me. It was a walk of shame I hope never to experience again.

Exiting the school and in route to the jail, I found my voice and asked the policeman, "What am I being arrested for?" I couldn't be sure, but I thought I heard him mumble something about the fight on campus the day before.

Arriving at the precinct, I heard my friends in a holding cell right next to the waiting room. They were yelling my name and goofing off; I suppose they were making the best of a bad situation. The policeman put me in the same holding cell with Tim and Calvin. I was surprised to see Randy Smith there too. Randy was one of our good friends, and he had been arrested for the fight at the Gotta Go, with no connection to the school incident at all.

There were five of us in that holding cell for two hours before being taken to the jail cell. We were each issued a black-and-white jumper, a pillow, and a blanket. When we got to the cell, surprisingly there were two guys in there that I actually knew—a couple of old drunks that always roamed the neighborhoods.

That first night was crazy. There were six of us to a cell, and each cell was connected to another. There was one free-standing toilet, a shower with a drain in the middle, and six bunks. There was no clock or windows; no way to see if it was day or night. All you could see were bars and a bright yellow light in the middle of the hallway. Randy and I played checkers and board games to pass the time. We played for hours, just talking and trying our best to make it through the night.

The food was terrible. I skipped the first two meals, thinking I would get out soon. But by nightfall I was starving. There was a white guy in the cell with us, and he gave me a peanut butter and jelly sandwich that he had saved from lunch. He and I sat up and talked for hours after everybody crashed. I couldn't sleep. My mind was all over the place: I didn't know what to think or feel. I didn't know when I would get out. I didn't know what I was being charged with. And I didn't know if my mother knew I was in jail. I was just lost.

That night as I lay in bed, one of the guys suddenly raised up in his bed and just stood there with his eyes closed. Then he slowly got out of his bed, walked over to the shower, and turned it on. He stood by it with his eyes closed, motionless, for several more minutes. I never moved or said a word. I squinted my eyes to make it seem like I was asleep and just watched him. After a while he started making movements with his hands and arms. I wondered if this man had lost his mind! It looked like he was doing a voodoo ritual or something. He danced around before jumping into the shower. It was very strange.

It was about an hour after that when I heard someone in the first cell yell, "Chow!" Breakfast was being served at five o'clock. I could hear the breakfast trays being passed out. There was a small hole in the door for our food to be pushed through. I didn't have much of an appetite, so I gave most of my food to "Dirty Red" in the adjoining cell. Dirty Red was my dad's neighbor's son. He played this game with me where he would call my name, "Bryant Ray," and I would answer, "What?" Then he would reply, "You got the same name as me." We'd laugh every single time as if it were the first time he'd said it. The truth was, we only had the same middle name.

The next day was December 6, 2006—my birthday. I never told the fellas. And since I never got to make a phone call, I didn't know if my mom knew where I was. My throat clenched as I held back unshed tears. The shame and sadness I felt about spending my birthday in jail was too painful. I kept quiet all day.

COMING HOME

I have learned that peace is not the absence of trial, trouble, or torment
but the presence of calm in the midst of them.

—Coach Don Meyer

By the third day in jail, I was tired and lonely. I missed my mom and my brothers. I wanted to go home. I jumped up every time an officer opened the doors. Every time I prayed they were coming to take me home.

Seventy-two hours crawled by before the judge set bail for us, and the court leisurely called us in for a demeaning walk down the corridors to be arraigned. Shackled and cuffed like condemned criminals, we walked in a straight line and were ushered into the courtroom. I squinted against the brightness as we entered. The muffled sounds of people whispering and shuffling filled the room, until we entered. Then the room got really quiet. At first my head was down, but as we entered, I looked up and saw my mom.

My heart raced as she started to cry.

As my eyes stayed fixed on her, all I could think was that she was there, waiting for me. For the first time in three days I had hope.

Moments passed before I noticed that other parents and family members had filled the courtroom. To my surprise, there were a lot of people from the community there as well. I had no idea our situation had caused such an uproar. Locked up in the cell, it seemed like the world had forgotten us.

23

The courtroom was cold. The worn wooden benches were hard and uncomfortable. Never having been in a courtroom, I was troubled by all the commotion and attention. It was hard to focus.

The judge, was an older man, around sixty-five years old. I didn't know much about him, but he looked old enough to remember when the town wasn't always white, but young enough to understand that the world could change. When he called the court to order, the sound of the gavel hitting the table sounded like a sonic boom. He then commanded us to stand up and state our name and birthday. Each time one of us stood up, the others on each side felt their hands raise just a little as the chain pulled up; it felt like we would never get out of there.

When my turn came, I stood up slowly. I had no feelings. I was innocent, and I still believed this was just a temporary misunderstanding. After I gave my name and birthday, the judge looked at me and declared, "You are being charged with attempted murder and conspiracy to commit attempted murder." Fear raced along my body, tightening my muscles and draining my heart. *Murder!? Who did I try to murder? When? How? Was it someone that looked like me? Then the charges were outstanding! Attempted murder for a school yard fight—I mean the kid only had a black eye?* I felt the charges would never stick. Seriously, if six guys of our stature were to jump one person, I believe the damage would have been a bit more severe.

As these thoughts raced through my mind, I saw Mom break down and cry. I stilled myself. I didn't want her to see how I felt, so I just stood there. For her sake and mine, I told myself to stay positive. After all, I was innocent. I had my share of fights and trouble in the town. But this was crazy. I had never tried to kill anyone.

After each of us had been arraigned, the judge set my bond at $70,000! That was more money than my family had seen in a lifetime—at least that's the way it seemed to me. After the arraignment, our shackles were checked, and we marched back to our jail cell. I didn't know what to expect next. The judge never said, and I didn't have an attorney to come in and explain things.

That night in jail, I could hear someone whimpering. I wanted to join them, but I had to stay strong for Mom. Randy and I talked about what had happened at school. Neither of us really knew what had happened or why we had been singled out.

The next morning, just as I was about to settle into the day's routine, a policeman came into the cell block. By this time, I had stopped hoping it was for me. I just kept playing cards. "Bryant Purvis," the officer called out. Shocked, I looked up to see what he wanted. "You made bail," he said as he opened the cell door to release me.

Dad and Mom were waiting in the hall. I could see the deep lines of concern etched on their faces. A flood of emotions filled my soul as they hugged me back to life. Dad didn't say much. Mom couldn't stop wiping away her tears. She held my hand as we checked in with the desk officer to get my belongings. Leaving the old building was like coming out of a nightmare. But little did I know this was only the beginning of the worst nightmare yet: living as a Jena 6.

Mom drove me to my aunt's home. I couldn't wait to eat a solid meal. I was grateful. I hadn't really eaten in days. We talked a little bit about the situation. It was good to see her. Her big hugs were moistened by tears. The four of us talked for hours. I told them everything I knew. After a while, Mom could tell I was exhausted and suggested we continue the next day.

It was good to be home. I took an extra-long shower; the stench from the jail was driving me crazy. Standing there, feeling every drop of water pound my skin, my thoughts kept replaying everything that had happened. It had all seemed surreal, almost like a dream.

HOPE DIES AGAIN

A person really doesn't become whole until he becomes a part of something that's bigger than himself.

—Jim Valvano

It was days later when we heard about the vote. All but one person on the school board committee had voted for all of the Jena 6 to be expelled. Marcus Gregor, a friend of my father's, said he voted against the ruling because he believed we didn't deserve to be expelled. "Everybody makes mistakes, and everybody deserves a second chance," he told the committee.

The committee disagreed.

I had spoken to Coach about playing the Friday night games. But since we had been expelled, I couldn't play. The school board committee had ordered us not to come to school or be on school premises. This, for me, was more devastating than jail. All I had ever wanted to do was play ball. It seemed I could overcome everything else—the lies, the injustice, the separation from my family—but taking away the games was too much! So that day, I left for Dallas.

Mom was afraid for me. It was my first time driving on the road by myself, and I had never traveled outside of fifty miles of my hometown alone. She tried everything she could to convince me to not drive, especially since the car was a beater handed down to me from my brother.

It was a '97 Honda Civic. My brother worked very hard on that car. Every paycheck he got from his job he would spend on that car. It had LED lights, 18" rims, and two 12" subs banging in the back. My brother had that little two-door Honda fixed up nice. That was until one day when a fire started in the car. He immediately called the police, but by the time they arrived, the car had suffered so much damage it was considered totaled.

Mom decided to keep it anyway, and I helped her clean and scrub all the damaged interior and strip the inside completely. After weeks of cleaning and stripping, we searched all the local junkyards to find matching parts for the car. We found pieces from all over. There were pieces too small, and parts too big, but I was determined to make it work, and I did. After three months, I finally had a decent car. At least I thought so. It still had a strong smoke smell and no AC…but no big deal. I had a car.

I drove with the windows down and kept a decent speed to catch a little breeze. I hated coming to a complete stop or hitting a red light because within seconds I'd start to sweat. But driving from Jena to Dallas was about a new start, another chance to make it as a ballplayer. Once again hope filled my soul.

Texas was not ordinary. My uncle lived there, and I was going to stay with him. But from the start, I knew I was in for something. Driving through the neighborhood was crazy. The houses were huge like in the movies! In Jena, houses were barely standing. I mean, I was a small-town country boy, and this was as close to Hollywood as I had ever been! It was kind of scary, but I could see myself living this kind of life.

There were integrated schools with interracial couples walking happily and holding hands. This was really a huge change for me. I was used to seeing white people look snobbish and ignore me. But here in Dallas, not only did these people speak to me, but they smiled and said "thank you." I was shocked! I wasn't in Jena anymore—this was an equal environment. They didn't see color or if you were rich or poor.

My uncle was more like a brother than an uncle. My grandmother passed away when he was fifteen, and he moved in with Mom and us. He worked hard and played hard, and eventually went to college to play football for Grambling State University. His amazing skills got him drafted by the Dallas Cowboys. This was his second year in the NFL. He and my mom both believed that being out here would give me a new start and a better chance to succeed and stay out of trouble.

Once I got settled in, I called my mom. I could hear in her voice she was glad I'd made it. She seemed calmer. We talked about what my next step should be. Mom came down a few weeks later to enroll me in school. I was so excited. This would be my fresh start.

So when the school board said I couldn't reenter school until the expulsion was overturned, I was devastated! Every glimmer of hope I had vanished. My life was over.

I got back on the road a few days later and headed back to Jena. I was down to nothing.

Back in Jena, life was hard. I couldn't go to school. I had no job and too much time on my hands. To say I felt doomed didn't even come close.

One day, while sitting on the couch wondering where I'd end up in life, I got a strange call. It was Coach Elvis Pike, an AAU coach from Monroe, Louisiana. He told me there was a school that would take me right away, but it was an all-boys private Christian institution with a tuition.

Once again life gave me hope and took it away in one breath. With my mom being a single parent, I knew we couldn't afford it. But I told Coach Pike I'd talk it over with Mom and get back to him. That night when Mom came home, I told her what he'd said. I couldn't read her face. I truly expected her to say it was too much and not to worry, something else would come along. But to my surprise, she said okay. We'd move forward with the school.

"Mom, how can we afford it?" I didn't think she fully understood the cost.

"You need to be in school. We'll visit the school and see what's what. Let me worry about the money."

I tried not to get too excited during orientation, but being back on a high school campus felt good. No matter how hard I tried to keep it at bay, hope kept springing up.

"Tuition is one hundred and sixty dollars a week," the school principal said.

Upon hearing his words, I felt the disappointment wash over me like muddy water.

"Okay," Mom replied. "When can he start?"

My mom was superwoman in my eyes. I never knew how she did it. I never asked either, but I was extremely grateful. I swore I'd make her proud of me again.

YOU'RE GOING TO MAKE IT ONE DAY

To go from where you are to where you want to be: you have to have a dream, a goal, and you have to be willing to work for it.

—Jim Valvano

Within a week, I had moved to Monroe with my mother's sister and started attending Excelsior Christian School. It was a Class C school. It had about twenty students in grades seven to twelve, and two teachers. It was weird. I couldn't really get with the tight clothes and tucked-in shirts. I was used to wearing the style of the time: big clothes draping off my body. But at Excelsior, we had to wear white-collared shirts with tan pants and black or white shoes.

We all had class together, which meant I sat with seventh graders. The teachers split their duties: one taught half the classes, and the other teacher taught the other half. We had an African math teacher visit us. He was hilarious. He always had a funny joke or did fake karate moves at students, and just had fun with us.

The most important thing for me, though, was that the school had a basketball team! Even with so few students, we were really good. In fact, Excelsior had one of the best teams in the state with the number four player in the country. He was a six-foot-four shooting guard that could fill it up! He could do it all: shoot from anywhere, dribble through anybody or a whole team, and even soar by and dunk. He was a man among boys.

Our coach let me practice with the team and was planning on playing me that day after practice. He said all I had to do was get my mother to move to Monroe, and I could play right away. If not, I wouldn't be eligible to participate.

Robbed of hope again, I knew Mom didn't have the funds to move, nor would she consider doing so. So that year I couldn't play, but the coach was nice enough to let me practice and travel with the team anyway. I learned a lot from being with them. It made me want to be better.

Every night for six months I practiced my ball handling in the street in front of my aunt's house. I worked at it before going to bed every night, determined to get better. A lady, who I'd seen a few times passing by, stopped one night to talk. "I see you out here every night working hard," she told me. "You're going to make it one day. Keep at it. If it isn't in basketball, it will teach you how to work for something, and it will make you a better man."

Those words stuck with me.

Monroe was a cool town. I met some good friends there, and I got really comfortable. Then one of my friends introduced me to his uncle who owned a club. We were eighteen, and we used to sneak into the club almost every night. We'd also hang out outside the club, listening to music and taking turns freestyle rapping.

I had another good friend who lived a few blocks from the school. We became really close, and we hung out all the time. I stayed at his house overnight sometimes during the week. I also saw a lot on the streets, and I learned a lot. I never got in much trouble or said much as a teen. I sat back and watched everybody. I grew up fast. My mother never knew about my shenanigans.

I lived in Monroe until the end of the school year. It was harder than I had expected to leave my new friends. The day after school ended, I promised to keep in touch with everybody, all of us expecting to see one another in the big leagues.

I didn't want to live in Jena anymore. So I returned to Dallas. When I got back, I settled in and waited. School would start soon. Another shot at basketball.

THE MARCH

Failure does not come from losing, but from not trying.

—Larry Brown

Mom didn't have the money to hire a private attorney so we accepted the public defender, David Hackerman. He seemed nice, at first. So many people attacked us at the time that everybody wanted to represent us. But we didn't know the difference between a court-appointed lawyer versus a real attorney, so we went with Hackerman. He was a cool guy. I didn't do much communication with him. Mom handled it all. The only time I saw him or heard from him was during court sessions.

The day of the hearing finally arrived. He suggested I wear a suit to court, be clean shaven, and have a fresh haircut. Mom and I drove to the courthouse. It took some time before everything was in place and the hearing got under way. It wasn't until the prosecuting attorney read the charges against me that I realized the scope of my predicament. The school committee had used everything they could to place me at the scene. After several minutes of legal talk, the judge rescheduled another hearing. I traveled back and forth every month for court for rescheduled hearings. Every month I would fly home; court would last fifteen minutes just for the judge to reschedule my arraignment. It took me almost a year to get arraigned and about seven court dates.

While this was going on, there were four guys still in prison. Their bail was set so high that the families couldn't afford the cost. Two of the guys had charges from both altercations—the Gotta Go incident and the school yard fight—making their bails almost double. I remember one of them had a bail set at $140,000. To a black family in Jena, Louisiana, that was more money than they would hope to see in a lifetime.

By now the Jena 6 had become national news. Our parents teamed up to do everything possible to set us free: They called. They emailed. And they reached out to news channels, celebrities, and national figures to bring attention to our case.

One day the Jena district attorney called my mother. He asked for a private meeting with me to discuss my charges. He said that if I came in and told him everything I knew, he would let me get off scot-free—no jail time, no more court dates. I would leave with a clean record.

On that promise, I left Dallas and returned to Jena to talk to him. So many things raced through my mind on that long drive back. I had a jumble of mixed feelings.

Walking into his office, I noticed he had a big, bright smile. He turn on his recorder and asked me my full name, birthdate, and age. He then asked me what I was doing lately. I told him about playing college basketball. We talked about sports for a while. Then things turned serious. He asked if I knew Marcus Bates. I told him yes. Then he asked how close we were. I told him we were friends. He asked where I was when the fight broke out. I told him I was walking up the stairs near the gym. He then asked if I had seen Marcus hit John. I told him no. "I didn't see anything, sir; I was walking to class when it happened."

That's when his demeanor changed. He said, "So you mean to tell me you didn't see anybody touch John Bleacher?!" When I said no, he turned bright red and slammed the table. "You can leave my office! Now!"

I got up, told him "Have a nice day," and left. I had a feeling this would happen. I had a feeling he wanted me to rat everybody out. I believed he knew I was innocent in this fight; he was just using me to try to solve the case.

My mother cried that day. She was tired of all the court hearings, the threatening calls, and the total disruption to our lives. But most of all she feared losing me for seventy years in prison. She got a lot of people to talk to me to let me know the severity of the situation. They all seemed to want me to point the finger because they were scared for me. They knew what I was up against, even though I was not guilty.

In reality I didn't know what happened that day in the gym, but even if I did, I would have never spoke of it.

Over the next several weeks, our plight gained more and more attention. Our parents started small: They made signs that read, "Justice for the Jena 6." They called radio stations. And they called family and friends to rally in front of the Jena courthouse.

People from all over the world came to help. A random white man came to Jena and started writing a story on us. He helped our parents reach out to the people that we needed to shed a bigger light on the situation. This guy cared so much about us and what was going on; he was at every event, meeting, and rally. He worked with our mothers and fathers and paved a way for us to reach justice. He treated us like one of his own; like we were his children he was fighting for.

The first protest had maybe twenty people in attendance. But that didn't stop them. Each week the numbers doubled. Eventually local news channels were showing up, and that's when everything started really getting the attention. After a few months the whole world knew. The Jena 6 were trending on every TV channel, in newspapers, in tweets, and on blogs. You couldn't turn on the television without seeing our faces splashed across the screen.

The black community really came together. Celebrities and activist gathered together. I was amazed to see the black community stand up and fight together as a whole.

Soon the big dogs got ahold of it and started making trips to Jena and holding small rallies in the churches around town. That happened for a few weeks. Then everyone agreed that September 20, 2007, would be the day they would march for justice through the streets of Jena.

I came home for a rally held by Martin Luther King, III, and Al Sharpton. It was in a small black church in Jena in a neighborhood we called Headstart Loop. The church was very small, probably fifty people could fit in there. That day it was packed. Every chair, every inch was filled with residents, reporters, and activists. We were in the front row. It was so hot and stuffy, we had to use the paper fans with the stick to get fresh air. Everybody was sweating.

As Al Sharpton began to speak, I could feel a drip of sweat rolling down my arm. He spoke about racism in Jena, about his plans to make sure the remaining boys were released, and about justice. The crowd went crazy! This was a big deal.

After the rally, they all took a photo of the five of us who were out of jail at the time. Marcus Bates was the only member still behind bars.

The news of it spread everywhere! Big-time TV and radio hosts rallied thousands of people from the South to Jena, along with so many other people across the nation. The radio host from Dallas brought in buses to shuttle people into Jena. At the time, I was in Dallas. But I heard they were expecting over a 100,000 people to descend upon Jena.

The night before the march, I flew into Jena. It seemed like every passenger on the plane was either with the news or some sort of activist. Everybody on the plane was talking about it. But no one noticed me. I put a hoodie over my head and headphones in my ears to avoid any conversation.

My mother picked me up from the airport. When we arrived in Jena, I expected the town to be packed. I was totally wrong. The town was empty. The white people in the town had closed down all of their businesses. Car dealer lots were empty. Jena had become a complete ghost town. The white townsfolk of Jena believed it was going to be a violent riot. They were scared. Most of them skipped town, waiting for it to all be over.

On the drive home, Mom told me about all the death threats and phones calls she was receiving. She said it had been going on for months, but she kept it from me because she didn't want me to worry. But she wouldn't be able to hide it from me anymore.

That night I got a firsthand taste of it. Several phone calls came in threatening us. One official-sounding guy called and asked to speak to Bryant Purvis. Mom turned the phone over to me, and the guy said, "I'm gonna kill you…you nigger. We know where you live!" It shook Mom up. These people not only had our phone number, they had our address as well. People were selling our personal information online.

The next day I was at the courthouse by seven in the morning. As I pulled up, an army of police officers, in just about every color you could imagine, with the biggest guns, weapons, and shields ever made, lined the steps of the courthouse. There were so many SWAT teams everywhere, it was hard to park.

When I finally got up to the courthouse, I was approached by a group of about fifteen men in black suits. They immediately surrounded me and escorted me around the courthouse. I discovered later that they were the Black Panthers.

Several news channels tried to interview me. The crowd kept growing. There were so many people out there that day, it was hard to see the streets.

Al Sharpton opened up the rally and started the protest in front of the Jena courthouse as two of the Jena 6, Calvin Jameson and myself, and our parents took the stage next to him. It was an incredible sight to see so many black people standing together for a common cause. I couldn't believe it!

After the speech, Marcus Bates's mother phoned him. A few minutes later, he asked to speak to me. I grabbed the phone. "What's up, bro? Where you at? What you doing?" I hadn't spoken to him in so long, I couldn't believe I had asked such stupid questions. I knew he was in jail; it just didn't dawn on me at the time. I was so used to our normal conversation.

"You know where I'm at," he laughed. We talked for a few minutes, and then the march started. Thousands marched with us through the streets of Jena, Louisiana. We marched and chanted, "No justice, no peace!"

It was powerful. I was at the front of the march, arms locked with Mom and Calvin. I remember looking back, and all I could see was an ocean of people. I could barely move. We marched to Jena High School and through downtown Jena.

We marched all through the small town until we ended up back on the steps of the courthouse. There was another march scheduled in Alexandria, Louisiana, about sixty miles outside of Jena. Cars were backed up for over twenty miles. It was bumper-to-bumper with buses, charters, and vans.

The march in Alexandria lasted a couple of hours. And when I got back to Jena, it was dead again. The streets were totally empty. It was hard to wrap my mind around it all. Just hours before, thousands of people crowded the streets, and now it was empty. The only part of town that had life was at the Ward Ten Baseball Park. A couple of artists had come down to perform. It was like a big party with free food and drinks, and everybody having a good time. It was a great way to end the event. That night I flew back to Dallas. I had to get back to my normal life.

THE AFTERMATH

What do you do with a mistake: recognize it, admit it, learn from it, forget it.

—Dean Smith

After the march, things changed immediately. A defense fund had been set up for us to pay lawyers and legal fees. I was very grateful. One day one of the guys jokingly posted a picture of himself on social media with money hanging from his mouth. Someone found it, and the whole thing got blown way out of proportion. People said it was from the defense fund, but in reality he had been working all summer because we wasn't allowed to go back to school, and was just bragging about the money he had earned. But that one act caused us all a lot of grief. We were being accused of stealing the money and buying gifts. We quickly learned that the media was looking for something to fan the flames in the public eye.

That year Calvin and I were invited to the Black Entertainment Television (BET) Awards to be presenters. I was honored. They wanted all six of us to attend, but we were the only two that could make the event in Atlanta, Georgia. Everybody who was anybody was expected to be there. They invited our parents too. Mom always watched BET. It was one of her favorite channels. I was hyped about the invite.

I loved music and fashion, so to be among the greatest icons of the industry was unreal. It was hard to believe I was really at the BET Awards. It was a dream come true. When we arrived, we pulled right up to the red carpet. Every media outlet was there to ask us questions about the Jena 6 and about our plans for the future.

BET gave us the honor of presenting the Video of the Year Award. That year, Kanye West won the award. Who would have known he would become one of my biggest inspirations. The crazy thing about it was that critics of the award show mocked our presentation, even though every word of it was scripted by someone else and given to us to rehearse! Every word I spoke in giving the award was written by someone else except the part where I added my deepest appreciation for my mother and my uncle for all they had done for me.

The rest of the event was amazing. I got to meet and hang out with a lot of people I had looked up to as a kid.

When the awards were over, life went back to "normal."

I joined the basketball team that year, and we were expected to do very well. We only had a few games left, and we had to win one or both to make the play-offs. By the end of regular season, all I could think about was winning these games. I was averaging a double-double, and our team was playing extremely well. That year would be the first year in my high school career as a basketball player to make the play-offs. I was on a mission. I wanted to feel that feeling.

So when I woke up late for school the morning of February 5, 2008, I was very angry with myself. Up until then, I had not gotten into any trouble, not even a tardy slip! And now I was rushing through traffic, trying to avoid being too late.

The school parking lot was full like always, and I only had five minutes to get to class. The lot was huge, so I always searched closest to campus before going to the back. It seemed like it took a mile to walk from back there. Passing by the cars, I found a parking spot up close in the front. I noticed a guy standing in the middle of the parking spot. I rolled down my window to ask him to move, but he spoke first. "You can't park here. I'm saving it for my girlfriend." But I was late, and it was a parking spot up close, so I pulled in. The guy stormed off as I got out of my car. I ran inside, barely making it to class on time.

That was the day of our first game. I was excited. It was district time, and we were fighting for play-off spots. After school, the team headed out for the road game. We rode about an hour away. A lot of parents and students followed the bus to the games.

After the game, some of my teammates rode home with their parents. I rode on the bus. Sitting there I got a phone call from a teammate saying that my car had been vandalized and my tires had been sliced. I couldn't believe the news. I thought it was some sort of joke. But when I got to my car, I saw the damage was real. *That biker kid*, I thought. The one I had run into that morning before school. That was the only incident I had had since moving to Dallas.

My uncle picked me up that night from the school. We left my car there. He asked me if I knew who could have done it. I told him what had happened that morning. We laughed about it, and he told me to forget about it.

But it just didn't sit well with me.

That next day I was angry. I had stayed up all night thinking about it. Back at school that day, I saw my car still there, damaged. It made me even angrier. The first thing I did that day was go to the principal. I told him that my car had been vandalized the night before. He told me it was a big parking lot, and it would be hard to see on the cameras who had actually done it.

Taking matters into my own hands, a couple of my friends and I were standing around before class, waiting for the biker guy. We saw him sitting with his girlfriend at a table not far from where we were standing. I went over and grabbed him by the back of the neck. I told him I didn't mess with anybody, and he'd better not ever put his hands on my car again. Then I pushed his head against the table and left. The whole school was gathered around, watching.

I knew I was in trouble.

I walked straight to the principal's office. Sitting there in his office, I asked myself why I lost my temper? I knew this would not make my situation any better. I really regretted what I had done.

The principal asked me what happened. I told him word for word what I had done. He said he would bring the biker kid in for questioning. I waited outside. But he never arrived. Instead, a police officer walked in and arrested me.

Once again I had to walk through the school with cuffs on. Here I was once again being arrested. I knew my mom and my uncle were going to kill me! I was supposed to stay out of trouble, not make it up as I went along.

LIVING WITH REGRET

Push yourself again and again. Don't give an inch until the final buzzer sounds.

—Larry Bird

At the police station, they booked me and then strip-searched me. The irony of it was that I had on a Jena 6 T-shirt under my regular shirt. I was told I could keep only one shirt and shorts. I chose the Jena 6.

With my one phone call, I called my uncle. Waiting for him to answer, I wondered how to break the news. He was very upset with me. I wasn't sure he'd be there for me this time. I sat in my cell, wondering about my life.

A call came over the intercom saying the judge wanted to see me. It was midnight. *What is a judge doing at the jail at midnight?* I wondered. She set my bond and charged me with assault causing bodily injury. Soon after that they shipped me out from Carrollton Jail to Denton County Jail. As I was being booked, the clerk told me my mother was there to get me, but I still had to go through the whole booking process all over again.

After the booking, they placed me in a holding cell with about fifty people. It was crowded. People were everywhere, sitting on benches, sleeping on the floor. Two guys were taking a dump on the free-standing toilet in the middle of the room. I found a corner and just sat there and kept to myself.

Two hours crawled by before they finally called my name. That ride home was silent and awkward for several miles. Then Mom spoke.

"Son, do you know you are on every news channel in America right now?"

"No, I didn't."

"What were you thinking?" .

I was speechless. When we got to my uncle's house, he drilled me for over an hour. I was in trouble with everybody. The blogs were insane. People were saying I was a thug, and that the march was a waste of people's time.

I knew I had really messed up.

For two weeks straight I woke up every day to reporters and cameras at my uncle's doorstep, wanting to interview me. It got really annoying. I felt even worse because my mistake was affecting my uncle's job. The news reporters were hassling him after work, trying to get interviews and asking him questions about me.

The school placed me on a ten-day suspension. I would miss our high school basketball play-off game. It was the first time I had ever earned a play-off spot. What hurt the most was that I would be leaving the team in a bind for the tournament. They lost that game by six points.

I returned back to school and was placed on probation for a year. I had to take anger management classes as part of my punishment. I eventually graduated without any more incidents.

Now I was searching for colleges. I was accepted into Ranger College in Ranger, Texas. I played basketball for two years with them and graduated with an associate's degree in science.

In late July, we were out for the summer. After more than two and half years, the Jena 6 case was finally coming to an end. The judge wanted to end the case, and the Bleachers had had enough. They were ready to move forward with their lives.

Mom called me and said it was over, and all we had to do was apologize, pay a fine, and do seven days probation. She said we would plead "no contest." She said a no-contest plea was not a guilty plea; it was an acknowledgement there was evidence of possible guilt, but it would resolve the case quickly. When I heard that I jumped on it fast. Knowing that I could possibly spend life in prison, I was happy to get it over with.

In court that day, we found out there was more to it than what we were led to believe. There were statements in the documents that supposedly said we had placed all the blame on Marcus Bates. When I heard the statements in the plea, saying that we had nothing to do with the situation and blaming it all on Marcus, I knew it was a false statement because I didn't know the truth; that is, who had hit him or who didn't.

Marcus pleaded guilty to second-degree battery as a juvenile in December 2007. During the case, the clerk reading the statements kept saying we were "guilty" instead of "no contest." One of our lawyers kept correcting her. I didn't feel comfortable because those were not my words. I was there when they were planning the conspiracy. I was among the crowd when everyone was making plans to start a black-on-white fight, but no one individual had been targeted. But I was not there when John was attacked. In the actual fight we were charged with, I didn't play a role in it. Nonetheless, I was accused and charged.

The criminal charges were reduced from attempted murder to second-degree battery—a felony that could have resulted in a $2,000 fine and up to five years in prison. In terms of the deal, we agreed to pay fines of $500 each and court costs of $500 each, with the exception of one, because he had spent seven months in jail, which was one more month than the maximum sentence for the misdemeanor charge.

We were put on unsupervised probation for seven days and ordered to stay away from John and his family. And, most important to them, we couldn't speak to the media. The district attorney opened up the meeting, saying, "The road to reach this day has been long and painful, especially for the victim in this case, John Bleacher, and his family. While I believe it would have been appropriate and possible to convict these defendants of felony offenses, this action today concludes the matter for John, and that is what we all wanted."

Then the clerk read our statement that they, the court, had created for us, the defendants. It read, "We hope our actions today help end this nightmare for John, Mr. and Mrs. Bleacher, and all others affected, including the town of Jena."

It was a hard thing to shake, especially knowing I had not attacked John that day.

My day in court happened the same day Michael Jackson died. I expected the news to be all about the court's decision, but everybody was so shocked in the passing of the pop king that the ending of our case went under the radar. It was kind of a relief. It was attention I didn't want.

Trying to put back the pieces of my life, I went on from there and played for Southeastern Louisiana University for a year, and then transferred to Grambling State University.

GRAMBLING

To be a great teacher of the game you must study the game; know your craft and be proud of your knowledge; but never satisfied with your knowledge.

—Kevin Eastman

Grambling State University started a new chapter of my life. As a historic black college university, it might not have been a good fit for me because of my past, but I made an effort to fit in. I went to the pep rally for the beginning of school orientation. The auditorium was packed as the president of the university got up and spoke about the history of the school and its faculty. The ceremony lasted about an hour, and at the end the committee gave everyone a lit candle. As I looked around, I could see hundreds of candles flickering in the dark auditorium. And as we sang the school anthem, at that very moment, goosebumps covered my body, and I felt like I was home. I had never experienced anything like that before.

Grambling quickly became the best place for me. They took me in with open arms, and I immediately felt accepted. There was so much history and tradition. I was proud to be a part of something greater than myself.

The year I started there, we believed we had the talent to play at maximum level and take our team to the tournament. We trained hard! I spent a lot of my free time in the gym working on my game. Before practice, after practice, and sometimes even after games.

College work was tough for me, and the gym was the only place I could go and unwind, and clear my mind. I loved it in there. I was always at peace.

As the preseason workouts came to end, just about every possible thing that could happen to a team happened. We lost three of our best players before the season could even start. We had five walk-ons and four scholarship players. We went 4–28. It was the worst year I've ever had as a basketball player. I went out every night and gave it my all. It was draining losing that many games. I thought about quitting so many times.

During the summer I trained hard. I ran and lifted weights. I shot more hoops than I had ever done before, determined to reach my goal as a professional. As the school year was approaching, I was bitten by a spider. My arm swelled up like a melon. The doctor drained my arm and gave me some meds. I thought that I was good to go, but after weeks of more training I started to lose weight rapidly. I lost my appetite, and I couldn't use the restroom. I had this extreme pain on my left side. I knew something was terribly wrong. I was at school, and the local emergency staff, after two visits, said that I just needed rest and was dehydrated.

After talking with my parents, I decided to get a second opinion. I immediately left for Dallas. I went straight to the emergency room. After hours of tests, they discovered the spider was carrying methicillin-resistant Staphylococcus aureus, or MRSA, and it had gotten into my bloodstream, shutting my body down. The doctor told me I should have been dead weeks ago and that I was a walking miracle. I had a mass on my kidney and severe dehydration. I was also constipated and hadn't used the restroom in almost a week. The doctor told me that being an athlete really helped me in this situation. He couldn't believe how my body had held up for so long. The MRSA had been in my bloodstream for almost a month.

I didn't have health insurance, and the medicine I needed cost almost $5,000. I had so much on my mind at the time. I thought I was going to die. I searched for a miracle. The doctor gave me the option of filling out some form for approval to get a procedure done for free. Hours later the doctor came in and said I had been approved, and I needed to go into surgery right away to remove the mass that was causing so much pain. The operation went well, and I was hospitalized for a week then bed rest for two. I eventually recovered and was ready to take on my senior year.

That summer my son Kenzo Von Purvis was born. I carried a full load. With the responsibilities of having a baby to care for, full classes, and basketball, I had days when it was really tough for me. But I adjusted. I managed my time, rarely having any free time. But I loved taking my son to school every morning after my five o'clock run. It was the highlight of my day. Then I had class until three in the afternoon, and practice from four till seven. I got home about eight every night. I came home to be a father, then I tackled my schoolwork until the late hours. It was rough, but I was determined!

On the basketball team, I made a lot of new friends. Some of them had heard about the Jena 6 and asked me questions. At first I was uncomfortable about it. I didn't want my life to be centered on that difficult period in my life. After a while I realized that it would always be a part of my life, and the best thing I could do was learn from it. I eventually became very open with the guys. I shared my story and talked about the struggles I had faced as a kid. Coach was hoping he could inspire or spark something in the guys.

I finished school a year later and graduated with a bachelor's degree in criminal justice and a minor in business management. It was a huge accomplishment for me and my family. I was the first person in my entire family to graduate from college.

I left Grambling and moved back to Dallas. At the time I was working for Achieve Higher Goals Now, a basketball skill-development program designed to teach kids the fundamentals and advanced skills necessary to become better basketball players. In the beginning, I only worked for the company during the summer months.

I loved working with the kids. I didn't have anything like that when I was growing up, so it meant a lot to be a part of something important to me. I gave the kids and the company all I had. I challenged them and worked to bring out the best in each of them. Two years later, I started working full time.

After Jena 6, it was always hard finding a job. The second-degree aggravated battery and assault charges still hung over my head. I would get all the way up until the interview process, then I wouldn't hear back...from anybody. It was frustrating at first, but I didn't give up. I told myself I wouldn't let this stop my dreams from coming true or let it define who I was as a person. I believed that getting a solid education would help turn things around.

One day I was at my uncle's house; he wanted me to go shopping for him for a trip he had coming up. He loved the new gear I picked out for him. He asked if I ever thought about becoming an image consultant. He said I had a great sense of style, and he knew a couple of potential clients that could use my assistance. It got me excited. We talked for hours about designing T-shirts, clothing-line names, shoes, and everything fashion.

I ran with that idea.

That night I went home and researched everything I could find on the subject of image consulting, fashion, and designing. I was eager to learn everything I could.

My first gig was just days away for a Dallas Cowboy. I was very nervous. Although confident in my skills, I realized that working with an actual client was scary. After meeting the guy and getting an idea of what style would work best for him, I dove right in. It took two days to pull all the items together. And when it was done, he was very happy. Word got around, and pretty soon I was styling a small group of guys. I had always wanted to be an entrepreneur, to be successful and make a difference in some way.

When I was styling clients, it made me feel good to make someone else look and feel good about themselves. Even cutting people's hair. It was a burning passion, but I never paid attention to it. Being around fashion and art brought out the best in me. It made me creative. It made me want to express myself in ways I never imagined.

From those small steps, my goal was to create an authentic clothing line that was fashionable, classy, and edgy. I wanted to make something that was dope, something that fit me, and something that told my story. In November 2013, I opened Checkmate. A name that told my story; a brand that meant something to me.

Checkmate means game over—you win! And just like chess, in life, it is all about the moves you make.

CHECKMATE